WASHINGTON
REDSKINS

BY BO SMOLKA

SportsZone

An Imprint of Abdo Publishing
abdopublishing.com

abdopublishing.com

Published by Abdo Publishing, a division of ABDO, PO Box 398166, Minneapolis, Minnesota 55439. Copyright © 2017 by Abdo Consulting Group, Inc. International copyrights reserved in all countries. No part of this book may be reproduced in any form without written permission from the publisher. SportsZone™ is a trademark and logo of Abdo Publishing.

Printed in the United States of America, North Mankato, Minnesota
042016
092016

Cover Photo: Matt Rourke/AP Images
Interior Photos: Matt Rourke/AP Images, 1; Tony Tomsic/AP Images, 4-5; Al Messerschmidt/AP Images, 6-7, 8, 18-19; AP Images, 9, 10-11, 16-17; Pro Football Hall of Fame/AP Images, 12-13; Bettmann/Corbis, 14-15, 22-23; David Longstreath/AP Images, 20-21; David Drapkin/AP Images, 24; Lawrence Jackson/AP Images, 25; Nick Wass/AP Images, 26-27; Alex Brandon/AP Images, 28-29

Editor: Todd Kortemeier
Series Designer: Nikki Farinella

Cataloging-in-Publication Data
Names: Smolka, Bo, author.
Title: Washington Redskins / by Bo Smolka.
Description: Minneapolis, MN : Abdo Publishing, [2017] | Series: NFL up close | Includes index.
Identifiers: LCCN 2015960453 | ISBN 9781680782370 (lib. bdg.) | ISBN 9781680776485 (ebook)
Subjects: LCSH: Washington Redskins (Football team)--History--Juvenile literature. | National Football League--Juvenile literature. | Football--Juvenile literature. | Professional sports--Juvenile literature. | Football teams--Washington (D.C.)--Juvenile literature.
Classification: DDC 796.332--dc23
LC record available at http://lccn.loc.gov/2015960453

TABLE OF CONTENTS

FAST FACT

Running back John Riggins was known as "The Diesel." When Riggins ran the ball at home games, a loud horn from a diesel truck would sound sometimes.

RUNNING TO GLORY

It was now or never for the Washington Redskins. They trailed the Miami Dolphins 17-13 in the fourth quarter of the Super Bowl on January 30, 1983. Washington faced fourth-and-inches at the Miami 43-yard line. The Dolphins' defense crowded the line of scrimmage. It was John Riggins's time to shine.

Joe Theismann, 7, quarterbacked Washington to the Super Bowl against the Miami Dolphins.

Quarterback Joe Theismann handed off to Riggins. He ran left. At the 40-yard line, Dolphins defensive back Don McNeal hit Riggins near his shoulders. Riggins was too strong and powerful to be tackled that way. He ran over McNeal and rumbled all the way down the sideline for the touchdown.

John Riggins shook off a tackle to score the touchdown that put Washington on top for good.

That touchdown gave Washington its first lead at 20-17. Later that quarter, Theismann hit receiver Charlie Brown for a score that put the game away. The final score was 27-17. For the first time, Washington was a Super Bowl champion.

FAST FACT

The Washington offensive linemen of the 1980s were nicknamed "The Hogs" for how they pushed opponents around. Some fans even wore rubber pig snouts to games.

Some Redskins fans made the trip to cheer on their "Hogs" at the Super Bowl.

Charlie Brown caught the final touchdown pass in Washington's first Super Bowl win.

SLINGIN' SAMMY BAUGH

The Boston Braves began play in 1932. The team changed its nickname to the Redskins the next year. Attendance was poor, so in 1937, the owner moved the team to Washington, DC. Success quickly followed.

One big reason was quarterback "Slingin'" Sammy Baugh. In his rookie season, Baugh led Washington to the 1937 National Football League (NFL) championship.

Slingin' Sammy Baugh, *33*, was one of the best quarterbacks in NFL history.

FAST FACT

Sammy Baugh was more than a great quarterback. In 1943, he led the league in punting and intercepted 11 passes on defense.

Over the next eight years, Washington reached the NFL title game four times. In the 1942 championship, the Redskins faced the undefeated Chicago Bears.

The Bears had demolished opponents, winning their final six regular season games by a total score of 199-14. None of that mattered to the Redskins. Led by Baugh and a strong defense, they won 14-6. They were NFL champions again.

FAST FACT

In the 1940 NFL Championship Game, the Bears clobbered Washington 73-0. It is the most lopsided game in NFL history.

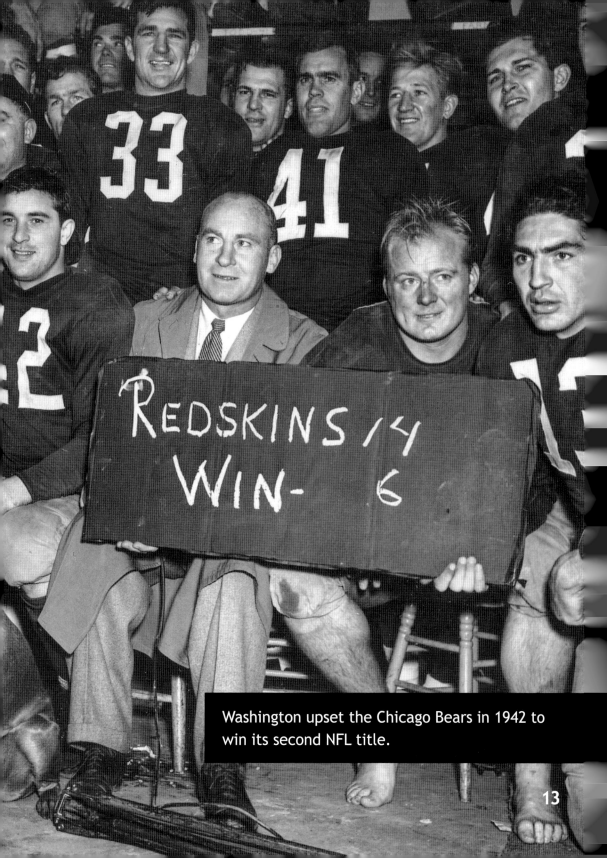

Washington upset the Chicago Bears in 1942 to win its second NFL title.

THE "OVER-THE-HILL GANG"

After the glory days with Sammy Baugh, Washington went 25 years without a playoff appearance. That changed in 1971 when George Allen was hired as coach and general manager. Allen chose to fill his roster with several older, more experienced players. They became known as the "Over-the-Hill Gang."

Five-time NFL champion coach Vince Lombardi coached Washington in 1969.

FAST FACT

Hall of Fame coach Vince Lombardi coached Washington in 1969, the team's first winning season since 1955. But Lombardi died just before the 1970 season.

FAST FACT

Quarterback Sonny Jurgensen and linebacker Sam Huff were Washington stars in the 1960s and 1970s. After their playing days, they became Washington radio broadcasters.

In 1972, The Redskins won nine straight games. In the conference championship game, they beat the rival Dallas Cowboys 26-3. They were headed to the Super Bowl for the first time. But the undefeated Miami Dolphins were too tough, and they beat Washington 14-7. It wouldn't be long, though, before the Redskins would be back in the big game.

Washington couldn't get past the undefeated Miami Dolphins in its first Super Bowl appearance.

FAST FACT

In the early 1980s, Redskins receivers would gather in the end zone after a touchdown for a leaping high-five. The group became known as "The Fun Bunch."

JOE GIBBS AND "THE FUN BUNCH"

Coach Joe Gibbs took the Redskins to new heights. From 1982 through 1991, they reached the playoffs seven times and the Super Bowl four times. Only in one season did they have a losing record. They won their first Super Bowl after the 1982 season.

"The Fun Bunch" was a huge part of Washington's success in the 1980s.

In 1983, Washington set an NFL record with 541 points scored. Joe Theismann, John Riggins, and wide receiver Art Monk were the offensive leaders of this era. All three players eventually made the Pro Football Hall of Fame. But they came up short in their return to the Super Bowl that season.

Theismann retired after the 1985 season. In 1987, backup Doug Williams filled in for injured starter Jay Schroeder in five games. Williams played well enough to be chosen as the starter for the playoffs, and he led Washington to another Super Bowl.

Art Monk has the most receiving yards in Washington team history.

21

FAST FACT

Doug Williams became the first black quarterback to start a Super Bowl. "Black America was watching me," Williams said. "[But] I was thinking about how to beat the Broncos."

The Redskins faced the Denver Broncos. Denver jumped out to a 10-0 lead. Then Williams took over the game. He threw four touchdowns in the second quarter. Washington rolled to a 42-10 win. Williams was named Most Valuable Player (MVP).

In 1991, quarterback Mark Rypien led Washington to another Super Bowl title. Gibbs won three Super Bowls with three different quarterbacks. That had never been done before.

Doug Williams celebrates after leading the Redskins to victory in the Super Bowl.

23

HARD TIMES AHEAD

Joe Gibbs retired after the 1992 season. Washington struggled to stay on top after that. It went 7-25 the next two seasons with two different coaches.

Daniel Snyder bought the team in 1999. In that time, he experimented with several coaches. There had been high-priced free agents that did not work out. By the 2010s, Super Bowl success was a distant memory.

FAST FACT

Hall of Fame cornerback Darrell Green played from 1983 through 2002. He stood just 5-foot-9, but he had blazing speed and toughness. He holds the team record for interceptions with 54.

Washington's current home, FedExField, opened in 1997.

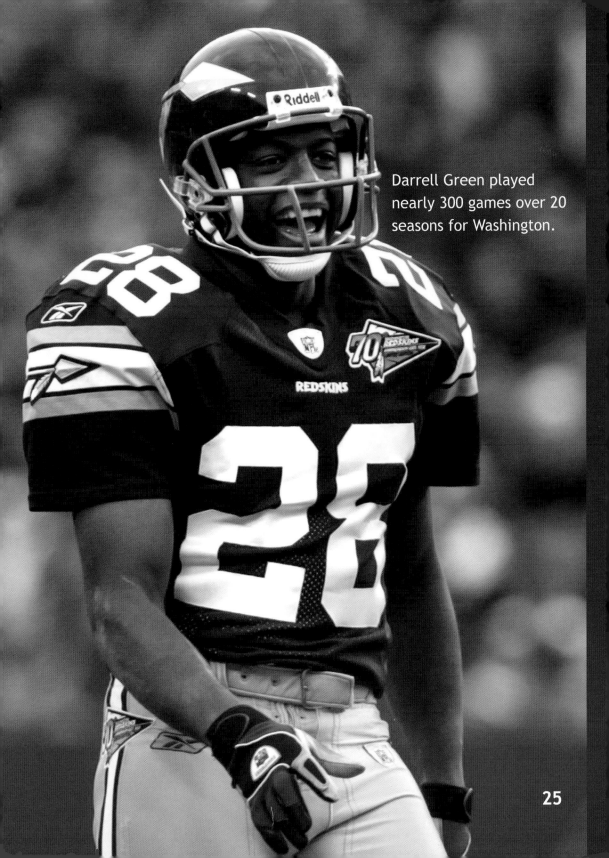

Darrell Green played nearly 300 games over 20 seasons for Washington.

FAST FACT

Washington is one of the few pro football teams with a fight song. It is called "Hail to the Redskins."

In 2012, the Redskins gambled on the future. They traded three top future draft picks to draft quarterback Robert Griffin III. "RG3" mania swept Washington. Griffin was electrifying when healthy, but he was slowed by injuries. The lost draft picks hurt the team's ability to rebuild.

Robert Griffin III was the 2012 NFL Rookie of the Year, but his career stalled due to injuries.

27

By 2015, Griffin was not playing much. Backup Kirk Cousins took over and led Washington back to the playoffs for the first time since 2012. Though it ended in a first round loss, Washington fans hope it is a sign of things to come.

Behind quarterback Kirk Cousins, Washington won its division in 2015.

TIMELINE

1937

The Boston Redskins move to Washington and win a championship their first season there.

1961

RFK Stadium opens. It is the Redskins' home until 1996.

1966

On November 27, Washington beats the New York Giants 72-41 in the highest-scoring game in NFL history.

1973

The Redskins play in their first Super Bowl on January 14. They lose to the undefeated Miami Dolphins, 14-7.

1981

Joe Gibbs is named Washington's coach. He leads Washington to the Super Bowl four times in the next 11 years.

1983

Washington goes 14-2, the best record in team history at the time. Joe Theismann is named the league's MVP.

1984

Receiver Art Monk leads the league with 106 receptions. He ends his career in 1995 with 940 catches, an NFL record at the time.

1996

The Redskins play their final game at RFK Stadium. They move to FedExField the next year.

2015

Washington wins its division for the first time since 2012 but loses in the first round of the playoffs.

GLOSSARY

ATTENDANCE
The number of fans present at a game.

DRAFT
The process by which leagues determine which teams can sign new players coming into the league.

FREE AGENT
A player who is free to sign with any team.

GENERAL MANAGER
A team employee who makes most decisions regarding the roster.

LINE OF SCRIMMAGE
The place on the field where a play starts.

PLAYOFFS
A set of games after the regular season that decides which team will be the champion.

RIVAL
An opponent with whom a player or team has a fierce and ongoing competition.

UNDEFEATED
A team that has lost no games.

INDEX

ABOUT THE AUTHOR

Bo Smolka grew up in Washington during the days of "The Diesel" and "The Fun Bunch." He now covers the Baltimore Ravens for Comcast SportsNet and is a member of the Pro Football Writers Association of America. He lives with his wife and two children in Baltimore and has written more than a dozen children's sports books.